SCHIRMER'S LIBRARY
OF MUSICAL CLASSICS

J. CONCONE

Op. 11

Thirty Daily Exercises
for the Voice

**These Exercises Form a Transition
from the Grand Style to the
Extreme Difficulties of Vocalisation**

For High Voice — Library Vol. 294

→ **For Low Voice — Library Vol. 555**

G. SCHIRMER, Inc.

DISTRIBUTED BY

HAL•LEONARD®
CORPORATION

7777 W. BLUEMOUND RD. P.O. BOX 13819 MILWAUKEE, WI 53213

T0051173

Thirty Daily Exercises

for

Alto.

Thirty Daily Exercises

for

Alto.

J. CONCONE. Op. 11.

In practising the following exercises, always endeavor to produce each tone with correct and pure intonation and uniform power. To this end, the exercises must be executed slowly at first, gradually accelerating the movement at each repetition, at the same time progressively augmenting the power of the tone. Practice conducted in this manner will infallibly lead to good vocalization.

3.

In order that the voice may be made to run through all the degrees of its compass, and thus acquire perfect evenness of the registers; each separate passage in the ensu-ing six exercises should be repeated several times before proceeding to that which follows it chromatically.

6.

8.

10.

Exercises in Triplets.

15.

16.

19.

20.

21.

22.

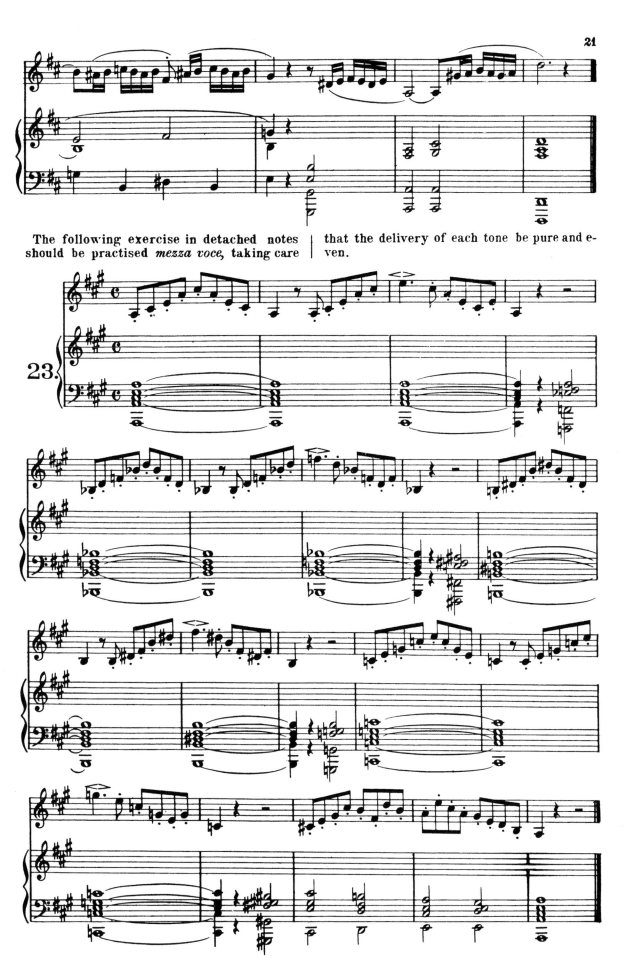

The following exercise in detached notes should be practised *mezza voce*, taking care that the delivery of each tone be pure and even.

Preparatory exercise for executing the Trill.

These graces called collectively Gruppetti, require the greatest distinctness of intonation combined with lightness; they are employed chiefly in the medium register. In the five following exercises the most common of these graces are given.

Exercises with same accompaniment as the preceding.

26. etc.

27. etc.

28. etc.

29. etc.

On the Chromatic Scale.

The diatonic progression of the major or minor scale is so natural, that even a person of mediocre endowments readily succeeds in producing, to any given tone, the six others separating it from its octave. This is not the case, however, when the succession is chromatic, *i.e.* progressing by semitones. The ear needs to grow accustomed to this less usual mode of progression, in order to vanquish a sort of repugnance which the voice feels to their easy and accurate execution.

It is the aim of the following exercises to prepare for conquering this difficulty;

one ought not to proceed to a new exercise before assuring oneself that the last can be well and correctly executed with respect to the accurate intonation of each tone. Nor should one practise self-deception as regards this good execution; it can be obtained only by dint of very considerable study.

In the exercises now following, the sign ∧ does not indicate a *rinforzando* of the voice, but a light rhythmical accent; a device, the high value of which will be speedily recognized, for the surer attainment of the goal.